MARKET YOUR SMALL BUSINESS ON A *Shoestring* BUDGET

Quick and Easy Tips to Help you
Save a Ton of Money on
Marketing and Advertising

by Craig Duswalt

Craig Duswalt International

Published by Craig Duswalt International

Printed in the United States of America

Duswalt, Craig
    Marketing Your Small Business on a Shoestring Budget / by Craig Duswalt
    ISBN: 978-0-9816008-0-2

Cover design and layout by Dawn Teagarden.

Photos by Gary Choppé.

For Natasha
my love & inspiration

For Tyler, Ryan & Hayden
my gifts from God

For Mom & Dad
my biggest fans

For Pamela & William,
Courtney, Taylor, Ashley & Michael
my support and prayer team

OTHER BOOKS BY CRAIG DUSWALT

MARKETING YOUR SMALL BUSINESS ON A SHOESTRING BUDGET

Quick and Easy Tips to Help You Save a Ton of Money on Marketing and Advertising

$12.95

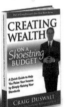

CREATING WEALTH ON A SHOESTRING BUDGET

Quick and Easy Tips to Help You Raise Your Income by Simply Raising Your Standards

$12.95

FUNDRAISING FOR YOUR NON-PROFIT ORGANIZATION ON A SHOESTRING BUDGET

Quick and Easy Tips to Help You Raise a Ton of Money for Your Non-Profit

$12.95

eBooks:

OUTSOURCING YOUR LIFE ON A SHOESTRING BUDGET

Quick and Easy Tips to Help You Spend Smart, So You Can Live Smart

$9.95

OUTSOURCING YOUR SMALL BUSINESS ON A SHOESTRING BUDGET

Quick and Easy Tips to Help You Work Smart and Spend Smart, So You Can Live Smart

$9.95

You may place your order online at www.CraigDuswalt.com

TABLE OF CONTENTS

ONE-HOUR BOOK SERIES

I created the One-Hour Book Series because I felt a need for small businesses to have a quick-tip, reference guide packed with great information, in a condensed, well-organized package so they could start saving a ton of money on marketing and advertising immediately.

Let's face reality. As much as I hate to say it, times have changed and everyone needs everything yesterday. I personally know that with running two businesses, raising three small boys, and spending quality time with my wife, it is virtually impossible to read a 300-page marketing manual. If I miraculously found time to read I'd rather read something inspirational.

All books in my One-Hour Book Series are designed to be read in about an hour, providing you with the tools needed to get started immediately, while at the same time allowing you that much-needed precious time to spend with your family and friends.

The One-Hour Book Series will grow to include guest authors writing Shoestring Budget books in their area of expertise. Enjoy the series, and more importantly, enjoy your life.

ABOUT CRAIG DUSWALT

Craig Duswalt is America's Shoestring Budget Coach and is the founder and author of the One-Hour Book Series and the Shoestring Budget books and seminars, which teach entrepreneurs, small business owners, non-profit organizations, performers and self-employed independent contractors how to market their business or themselves on a shoestring budget. He currently shares his Shoestring Budget System to audiences across America and has published his first set of books including, *Marketing Your Small Business on a Shoestring Budget; Creating Wealth on a Shoestring Budget;* and the eBooks, *Outsourcing Your Life on a Shoestring Budget; and Outsourcing Your Small Business on a Shoestring Budget.*

As an entrepreneur and President and CEO of Craig Duswalt International, Craig has developed an entertaining way to teach how to create wealth and save a ton of money on marketing and advertising. He is an energetic speaker who uses a unique mixture of principles and entertainment to help his audiences achieve the success they desire.

Craig worked closely with the bands Air Supply and Guns N' Roses on numerous world tours and was an award-winning screenwriter. He is also an award-winning copywriter, working as a senior copywriter for a Los Angeles-based ad agency until opening up his own shop, Green Room Design & Advertising, which was named the 2002 Santa Clarita Valley Chamber of Commerce Small Business of the Year.

Craig Duswalt served as the Producing Artistic Director of a professional Equity-Waiver theatre in North Los Angeles and opened his own professional theatre a few years later. This is where Craig created his Shoestring Budget System. Using this "system" the theatre became an immediate success.

Craig and his wife, Natasha, a recent cancer survivor, own and operate Peak Models & Talent, a modeling and talent agency in Los Angeles. In only ten short years this very small business has become a multi-million dollar success story with more than 1,000 clients and representing more than 300 models and actors. Again, part of Peak Models & Talent's success is directly attributed to using the techniques of Marketing on a Shoestring Budget.

Craig and Natasha have three boys: Tyler, Ryan and Hayden.

INTRODUCTION

Marketing Your Small Business on a Shoestring Budget is jam-packed with all the information you need to successfully market your products or services. I understand that most small businesses are launched on a shoestring budget and that marketing dollars are hard to generate, so I took all my years of advertising agency experience and chose what I felt were the most important tips to help your small business save money immediately.

From knowing your customer to using the Internet to increase sales; from writing a marketing plan to negotiating with your printer; from inexpensive logos to popular gimmicks, I reveal where you need to invest your dollars and where you can get the same impact for much less.

You don't have to pay big bucks for marketing and advertising anymore. You just need to be creative. You need to know what the pros know and how to get the most bang for every buck.

As a former ad agency owner, I know every nook and cranny of the business. I can tell you where to spend and where to skimp. I wrote this book to help shoestring businesses "stretch the shoestring." It's a quick read, and if you put my advice into action you can have top-quality marketing and advertising on a shoestring budget.

CHAPTER 1

STARTING YOUR SMALL BUSINESS

DEVELOP A COMPANY BUSINESS PLAN

Every business, large or small, should develop a detailed Business Plan. Think of a Business Plan as your vision formalized on paper. Write it, ponder it, refine it. But get it down on paper. You'll be amazed at how the process of forcing yourself to answer hard questions will help you shape a sound business.

A good Business Plan will serve as your roadmap to success, keep your eyes focused on the prize, keep your priorities and expenditures on track, and help you attract investors and financing. See Appendix A for a detailed outline of a Business Plan.

Cost: Zero – you should be able to do this yourself, with a little research on the Internet.

DEVELOP A
DETAILED MARKETING PLAN

Having marketing vision is essential when starting a new business. But vision without a specific action plan is a ship without a rudder.

Developing a Marketing Plan that includes specific goals, vehicles and budgets offers significant advantages. Planning six to twelve months ahead gives you a broader, long-term perspective of your marketing needs and expenditures, and allows you to take advantage of volume discounts on advertising space, services and printing. When you can commit to a schedule in advance you may also be able to negotiate longer payment terms.

But most importantly, a detailed Marketing Plan will help you stay focused on your brand goals and avoid purchases that aren't in your company's best interest.

See Appendix B for a detailed outline of a Marketing Plan.

Cost: Usually very expensive, but you can always get a sample Marketing Plan and create yours using their model.

MODEL YOUR COMPANY AFTER SUCCESSFUL COMPANIES...

Whether you're just starting a business or restructuring one, it's always wise to research similar companies. Identify what they did right and what they did wrong. Learn from their mistakes and you'll save yourself years of expensive trial and error. Find your own way to emulate what they did right without "reinventing the wheel."

You can find information about other businesses on the Internet as well as at your public library.

...AND AT THE SAME TIME DIFFERENTIATE YOUR COMPANY AND PRODUCTS

The trick to differentiating your company and products from the competition is identifying and aggressively marketing the thing that separates you from the pack...

- If you're a professional speaker, offer free eBooks to everyone that attends your seminars.
- If you're a dentist, offer a free exam and cleaning to be auctioned at a local charity event.
- If you're an accountant, offer a free tax consultation to your existing clients.
- If you're a financial advisor, hold free seminars to inform customers of a new service and serve a free continental breakfast.

Cost: This will usually just cost your time, and maybe a breakfast.

Marketing Your Small Business on a Shoestring Budget

CHAPTER 2
YOUR AUDIENCE

KNOW YOUR CUSTOMER INSIDE AND OUT

If you can answer these six questions chances are you have a successful small business:

1. Where does your customer network?

       National conventions and trade shows

       Local trade shows

       Community and civic events

2. What associations does your customer belong to?

       Business and professional groups

       Community and civic groups

3. What does your customer read?

       Trade magazines and newspapers

       Consumer magazines

       Special interest magazines

       Internet news sites

       Local and/or city newspapers

       Community papers

       Newsletters, both print and e-mail

4. How does your customer like to be contacted?

       Phone calls

       E-mails

       Letters

       In person

5. How did your customer first hear about you?

> Affiliate program
>
> Referrals
>
> Marketing
>
> Word of mouth

6. Why does your customer buy from you?

> Product quality
>
> Service quality
>
> Brand quality
>
> Your reputation in the industry
>
> Community relationships

Cost: Just a
little research.

KNOW WHAT YOUR CUSTOMERS BUY AND WHY THEY BUY IT

First of all your customers buy you. They buy you, they buy your style, they buy who answers your telephone, they buy your employees, and they buy your customer service.

They buy solutions to problems; they buy benefits, not features; they buy results, not promises.

They also buy:

- Credibility – you'd better have some.
- Guarantees – they do not like risk.
- Honesty – dishonesty will kill the sale.
- Brand Names – remember to be consistent in your branding.
- Word of Mouth – measures the public's acceptance of your product or service.
- Prestige – everyone wants to associate themselves with success.
- Value – do not confuse value with price.
- Hope – mainly for themselves.
- Convenience – an easy shopping experience without confusion.
- Selection – plan your line carefully.
- Success – raise your standards.

> Cost: Nothing, I just told you what your customers want.

WHAT MOTIVATES YOUR CUSTOMER TO BUY

How will your product or service benefit your customer? Be specific. You must be able to rank these benefits in order of importance to the customer.

Your suppliers often provide lists of product features. Look at each feature and convert it to a benefit. For example, a freezer may have the feature of being self-defrosting. The benefit to the customer is that he or she never has to empty and defrost it. Know your customer's strongest objections. What obstacles are delaying or preventing a purchase? Develop a strong reason why they should buy *right now*. Turn every missed sale into an opportunity to clinch the next one by learning why the customer didn't buy. Then find a benefit or other reason to counter that objection.

Cost: Free

KEEP YOUR CUSTOMERS

As a small business one of your most powerful competitive advantages is your ability to develop and retain strong relationships with your customers. The big boys can't compete in this regard. And customers love it.

Remember: *It's a whole lot cheaper to keep an existing customer than it is to get a new one.* Dedicate yourself to customer retention. Pay special attention to the top 25% of your customer base. Stay in touch with your customers. Be sure to demonstrate how much you appreciate their business.

Acknowledge their birthdays, anniversaries and successes. Reward loyal customers with value-added services and other special "loyalty" bonuses. These small tokens of appreciation don't cost much and your customers will remember it.

Cost: Okay, maybe take a client to lunch or dinner once in a while. It'll be the best money you ever spent.

USE SURVEYS AND QUESTIONNAIRES TO PINPOINT CUSTOMER MOTIVATIONS

Surveys and questionnaires are commonly used as an integral part of market research to collect data that is specific and crucial to the success of a small business. Develop a customer questionnaire that will provide clues about how your customers think and what motivates them to buy. You can even get a few clues about personality types from their hand-written responses!

Cost: The cost of paper and a pen.

BUILD YOUR DATABASE

Get as many e-mail addresses as possible and stay in touch with your customers on a regular basis. There are many creative ways to entice people to "opt-in" on your website – give away a free eBook; offer a free educational mini-course; hold a sweepstakes drawing that requires registrants to provide you with their e-mail address.

If you're speaking at an event collect everyone's business card in a bag and have a drawing where you give away one of your products or services. You now have everyone's e-mail address.

Keep in mind, to avoid being labeled a "spammer" you can only e-mail to people who have actively chosen to receive your mail.

Cost: You need a website and an inexpensive autoresponder – worth every penny.

CHAPTER 3
CREATE YOUR BRAND

BUILD A UNIQUE BRAND IDENTITY

Nothing is more critical to success than branding your company, your products and yourself—from day one.

Spend time crafting your name, building your public image and communicating your brand message. And every brand should have a unique logo and a consistent look. Your logo will be everyone's first impression of your brand.

You can often hire a graphic designer to create a really good, really inexpensive logo on certain websites, such as Elance.com. Design schools and community colleges that offer classes in design are another good source of talent. Most have a bulletin board where you can post your project. An ad agency logo will typically cost you at least a few grand.

Cost: You can now get a very good logo for between $50 and $100, and maybe even less.

STAMP YOUR LOGO
ON EVERYTHING

There's a reason that major household brands spend millions of dollars on advertising. One of the keys to successful branding is consistency in message and image.

Everyone in the world knows the McDonalds brand, yet McDonalds continues to bombard us daily with ads. The result? We can't possibly forget (or ignore) the McDonald's brand. We remain convinced that McDonald's is still relevant, and still The Leader.

Imprint your logo on everything: Every printed piece, display ad and promotional ad. Don't forget specialty items, such as coffee mugs, t-shirts or magnetic car signs.

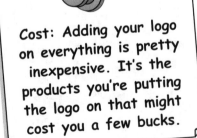

Cost: Adding your logo on everything is pretty inexpensive. It's the products you're putting the logo on that might cost you a few bucks.

DO NOT SKIMP ON
YOUR BUSINESS CARDS

Nowadays, we take business cards for granted, but they're still the single most essential—and least expensive—tool in your marketing arsenal. Print lots of cards and sprinkle them around generously. They're handy to carry and easy to offer.

Spare no expense in creating your business card. Make sure your card represents your corporate image and conveys your brand personality. It will be the one tool you'll use at every turn, and in many cases, the first impression a prospect has of your business.

Business cards have higher odds of being "saved" than any other single promotional tool you can offer. And your card provides instant contact information even if the person who receives it doesn't need it immediately. Consider putting your favorite motivational quote on the back of the card—giving the recipient another reason to keep your card on file.

At my modeling and talent agency, Peak Models & Talent, we get our business cards printed for free. How? I refer our models to various printers to get their ZED cards printed. Be creative! There's always a way to barter.

> Cost: Very minimal. And there are so many Internet sites that will print your first set of cards for free.

ALWAYS COMMUNICATE A CONSISTENT BRAND MESSAGE

Don't tinker with your brand message in advertising campaigns. Marketers often make the mistake of changing a brand once it's been on the market for a while. Don't do it. Take a lesson from the "New Coke" debacle. Follow fads and you'll destroy your brand.

Muddled marketing campaigns are the single greatest waste of promotional budgets—always have been. And inconsistency is not only expensive in terms of production expense; it costs you impact, as well as the trust of customers who have expectations of your brand.

Identity confusion is an unforgivable sin.

Cost: This will only cost you more money if you decide to change your image midstream. So stick with it.

DEVELOP EFFECTIVE PROMOTIONAL CAMPAIGNS

I used to get paid a lot of money to design ads and write press releases. But the good news for you is that there are more inexpensive sources of advertising talent than ever before. You can hire very good, professional freelance writers and graphic designers at Elance.com or Guru.com for about the price of a weeks worth of Starbucks.

Cost:
Prices vary
per project.

DEVELOP TIMELESS PROMOTIONAL PIECES

Write with vision. Imagine how your words will be perceived and interpreted two years from now, five years from now. Don't use language that will date your piece and require you to reprint a year later. For example, instead of using a phrase such as "Our company is ten years old," say: "Our company was founded in 1998."

It's usually not a good idea to include employee photos in your static promo pieces. Employees come and go. And some don't go under the best of circumstances. Two years from now you surely don't want to be stuck with the photo of an employee you fired for embezzling!

Recreating your static promotional pieces every year is a profit-killer.

Cost: If you spend money here you didn't read this tip.

WRITE GREAT HEADLINES

Write your ad knowing that everyone will do their best to *not* read it. Your challenge is to make the headline so irresistible that they simply must read the whole ad.

Hire good copywriters if you need to. But if you want to try your hand at copywriting here are a few tips:

- Headlines must either convey an idea or entice the reader to keep reading. You want them to *keep reading*.
- Speak directly to the reader, *each* reader, even if a few million people will read your headline. Keep the tone personal, not "mass market." Imagine that *you* need your product. On any given day, there will be prospects that want exactly what you have to offer.
- Experiment with newsy headlines that begin with "Announcing…" Use language that has an announcement feel.
- Experiment with headlines that begin with "New." Demonstrate why new is better.
- Include a date in your headline.
- Showcase the price—if you're proud of it. It doesn't necessarily have to be the lowest price for the ad to succeed.

- Demonstrate how affordable your offering is. Emphasize easy payments, long-term economy, reduced price, or the classic, timeless nature of your product.
- Announce a free offer.
- Reveal inside advice that has genuine value to your reader, proving your expertise.
- Be a storyteller.
- Begin your headline with "How to…"
- Begin your headline with "How," "Why," "Which," "You," or "This."
- Write a testimonial-style headline.
- Write a one-word headline.
- Warn the reader not to delay purchasing.
- Direct your message to the Maybes, not the Yeses or Nos.

Cost: Free—I just showed you how to write a headline.

WRITE COMPELLING BODY COPY

Headlines may engage readers but body copy must tell the story and convince the reader to stick around until the end.

Some tricks to try:

- Be specific, don't speak in generalities. Be a specialist who has inside knowledge.
- Keep it tight. Short paragraphs, short sentences, short words. You'll increase the odds that your full message will be read.
- Quote powerful one-liners from testimonials; ringing endorsements, personal expression of appreciation.
- Never speak down to your reader. Assume your reader is intelligent—most of the people who will actually finish reading your entire message will be.
- Use strong visuals to enhance and color your words. Photos, illustrations, diagrams, charts, graphs. And don't forget to add captions to photos that require clarification. People like photos. And clarification.
- Always have a call-to-action.

Cost: Very inexpensive on Elance.com or Guru.com.

Marketing Your Small Business on a Shoestring Budget

ALWAYS USE GOOD MARKETING WORDS IN YOUR HEADLINE OR BODY COPY

ADVICE

ALTERNATIVE

ANNOUNCING

BENEFITS

COMFORTABLE

DISCOVER

EASY

FREE

FUN

GAIN

GOOD-LOOKING

GUARANTEED

HAPPY

HEALTHY

INTRODUCING

LOVE

MONEY

NEW

NOW

PROUD

PROVEN

RESULTS

RIGHT

SAFE

SALE

SAVE

SECURITY

TRUSTWORTHY

VALUE

WANTED

WIN

WINNINGS

YOU

YOUR

Cost: These words are free—you can find them in any dictionary.

NEVER USE BAD MARKETING WORDS IN YOUR HEADLINE OR BODY COPY

BAD	HARD
BUY	LIABILITY
CONTRACT	LOSS
COST	OBLIGATION
DEAL	ORDER
DEATH	SELL
DECISION	TRAIN
DIFFICULT	WORK
FAIL	WORRY
FAILURE	WRONG

Cost: It won't cost anything if you don't use them. If you do use them, shame on you!

USE DIRECT MAIL POSTCARDS TO INCREASE RESPONSE

Using a postcard for a direct mail piece can increase your response rate *and* save you big bucks. I once read that color postcards can increase readership by as much as 41 percent and raise a prospect's inclination to purchase by up to 26 percent. Consider bulk mailing through a direct mail house. Or ask your local Chamber of Commerce if you can insert your flyer or postcard in one of their monthly mailings.

Always use either a 5 1/2" x 8 1/2" OR a 6" x 9" postcard because they are more effective than if you use a 4" x 6" postcard. It's also harder for potential clients to throw the bigger postcards away.

Cost: A little bit of money here. You have to print the postcards and then you have the cost of mailing them. Try bartering with the printer to get it for less.

EXPLORE THE VERSATILITY OF SALES LETTERS AND FLYERS

Sales letters and flyers allow you to present more detailed information about your product. And they're versatile—you can distribute them via e-mail, snail mail or fax. They're inexpensive to reproduce in bulk, especially black-and-white flyers or flyers printed on colored stock. Small print houses, for example, offer economy duplication services.

Cost: Basically the cost of photocopying. If you use e-mail, then once again, free.

CAREFULLY CHOOSE PROMOTIONAL ITEMS

Items such as pens, t-shirts, hats, and golf tees can be used as "bribes" to:

- Get a prospect to request your brochure.
- Get a prospect to accept a sales call.
- Reward someone for being a new or repeat customer.
- Get people to complete a survey.
- Motivate prospects to buy.
- Motivate people to increase their purchase.
- Increase morale, sales, safety, attendance and more.
- Build brand name awareness.

Here's an idea—get a rubber stamp and have your logo, tagline and contact information imprinted on it. Stamp everything you possibly can (where legal, of course).

There is a website called cafepress.com where you can create and sell a variety of customizable products with zero upfront costs and zero inventory investment.

Cost: Some of these items can get a little pricey. Choose carefully and select an item or two that is relevant to your business.

RECYCLE AND REPRODUCE YOUR MARKETING MATERIALS

Recycle a brochure panel into a display ad. Enlarge the cover into a poster, sign or kiosk. Don't worry about paying $100 for a photograph. If you can recycle that photograph for ten different applications each year for ten years your effective cost is $1 per use. A tiny investment and a wise one.

Cost: Set-up costs are usually what make a job expensive. If print material has already been printed it will usually be less expensive to print it again.

A GANG RUN WILL SAVE YOU BIG BUCKS ON PRINTING

Talk to your printer about adding your print job onto a gang run, which is on a large color press run. This can save you a nice chunk of change especially if you're printing four-color. The downside? You may have to wait a little longer to get your finished product and your color might be a bit off. Get a professional opinion on the quality issue from your printer. Chances are, it's well worth the small risk.

Cost: This price depends on the printer and how long you're willing to wait. Use your negotiating skills here. There is never a set cost in printing. There is always a way to pay less. They all want the job.

GIMMICKS

Gimmicks can be an inexpensive way to get noticed. The trick is to be clever, not "cheesy." Your goal is to devise a gimmick that's impossible to resist. Not only will you have a receptive prospect, you'll be admired for your cleverness.

Here are some examples of successful gimmicks:

- A home remodeling business mails photo postcards of a recent remodel to homeowners. The postcard features two shots: Before and After (in gorgeous color, of course).

- A mailing includes a reprint of your newspaper ad with a Post-It attached. On the Post-It is a hand-written note: "Craig, try it. This works! ~N."

- Give away money. Send a crisp, new dollar bill in your mailing to symbolize the revenue you can bring to your prospects.

- If you serve coffee imprint mugs with your logo. Honor a few repeat or big-spending customers each month by hanging their own mug on a rack.

- When you plan seasonal decorations look through catalogs such as *Oriental Trading—Business Edition* for related items. Send them to your customers with an invitation to see the new décor, hang their ornament on the Christmas tree, or whatever is appropriate.

Here is a great gimmick I implemented at one of my theatres: I created a fundraiser for the Santa Clarita Repertory Theatre called the Non-Benefit/Benefit where our 250 season ticket holders would have the option of paying $1,000 to see the President of the Board of Directors recite eight hours of Shakespeare monologues in his living room, OR donating $25, $50 or $100 to stay home in their comfortable house and NOT have to come to see him perform. Our expenses were minimal and we raised about $10,000.

Cost: Depends on the gimmick.

Marketing Your Small Business on a Shoestring Budget

CHAPTER 4
INTERNET
AND E-MAILS

LET THE INTERNET HELP YOU

You can find almost any information you need on the Internet. You can identify your competitors easily. Just search for the products or services you provide. If you want to learn about local competition, add "+your city name or state name" in your search. You can see where they are, what they offer, how they present themselves to customers and even what specials they are offering.

You can find statistics relevant to your industry or profession; research reports; trends and forecasts. Many industry-wide associations have websites with this type of information; you can also search directly for what you want to know.

You can find suppliers and quickly learn about prices and special offers in the same way you found your competition. Some industries, like printing, are highly competitive. You may save a bundle by using an out-of-town printer.

If you buy in large quantities from wholesalers consider going directly to an importer, or even importing yourself. You can find all the information you need on the Internet.

You can get good information on marketing and other business topics by taking advantage of the free newsletters sent by companies who hope you'll eventually buy an expensive course.

Cost: I'm sure you are already connected to the Internet, however, if you're not, you need to get Internet service and that will cost very little per month. Consider getting Internet access bundled with your cell phone service. You will never have to hunt for a Wi-Fi location again.

GET A WEBSITE

In this day and age, if you don't have a website for your small business, you're pursuing a hobby, not a full-fledged business. Shoppers look for products and services by searching on the Internet. If you're not there, they won't find you. And I'm not just talking about kids, either. Even elderly people use the Internet for shopping. People are too busy to call around looking for what they need.

Having a website doesn't mean you're going into competition with national discounters. It does mean that the dozens or hundreds of people in your town who are right now typing just what you offer into their search engine will find you among the results.

Numerous websites have templates you can use to design your own website. If you want to take orders over the Internet, they handle that, too. The monthly fee can be very inexpensive, depending on the services you buy from them.

Cost: You can get website templates for less than $100. Adding content is rather easy to do yourself. If you want to outsource that, like I do, hire an inexpensive junior graphic designer at a local community college. Elance.com also offers inexpensive web design services.

OPTIMIZE YOUR WEBSITE FOR EFFECTIVE PROMOTION

Maintain consistency between the look and feel of your website and your ad campaigns. Have other relevant websites link to your site, build goodwill in your niche, and prove to the search engines that you have stature in your community. Write a new search engine optimized article or two each month to boost repeat traffic and to help generate new (and free!) search engine traffic.

Be sure your website includes a positive-response opt-in box. You don't need to ask for a lot of information—just an e-mail address. You will need this to follow the rules about spam when you send autoresponders or other e-mail promotions.

Post articles on article directory sites to drive traffic to your website. Be sure to include your sound bite and website URL in your author resource box.

Cost:
Just your time.

GET LINKS, LINKS AND MORE LINKS

Contact owners of related websites and request a free link to your website. Offer to contribute articles in your area of expertise, which of course, would include your author bio with a link to your site. Write articles that provide valuable advice to the reader and you'll establish instant credibility as an expert while pre-selling your products.

While inbound links are only one factor in search engine optimization, "link popularity" can help boost your PageRank and relevance in the eyes of the search engines. And besides, every visitor who clicks through to your site is a potential customer. You can't beat free traffic!

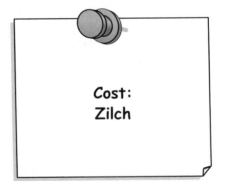

Cost:
Zilch

ATTACH YOUR BUSINESS CARD TO EVERY E-MAIL

.SIG files can automatically append themselves to the bottom of every e-mail you send, like little digital business cards. Be sure to include your logo, title and contact information—including your telephone number. Make it easy for people to contact you.

Also, add your blog address and any specials you might be having in your .SIG files.

Cost:
Once again, free.

LET AN AUTORESPONDER DO THE WORK

An automated e-mail series is an effective (and dirt cheap!) follow-up communication strategy that keeps your name in front of your customers for little effort. Load your autoresponder with an educational 5-day mini-course and let it rip.

Cost: Included in a good shopping cart system where prices vary.

SOCIAL NETWORKS, DISCUSSION LISTS, FORUMS, MESSAGE BOARDS AND NEWSGROUPS

Actively participate in relevant online communities. It's a great way to build brand awareness and establish your personal credibility. Don't forget to use a signature that promotes your products and points people to your website.

Social networks are free and they are a means to connect with friends and business associates around the country and even around the world.

The most popular social networks are MySpace, Facebook and LinkedIn. Others include Squidoo, Digg, Xanga and Bebo. You can include your personal information to meet like-minded people, and business information to network with potential customers.

Cost:
Free, free, free.

CHAPTER 5
SALES

GUIDE YOUR CUSTOMER TO THE CLOSE WITH "SOFT STEPS"

The soft step is a strategic pre-sell tactic that "softens up" your prospect and puts you one step closer to a sale. Soft steps build rapport, overcome objections and soften purchase resistance. You'll find that soft steps make it easier to guide your customer, step-by-step, to the close. Devise soft steps that will lead you directly to the hard step.

The ideal soft step costs you little or nothing, but has genuine value to your prospects. For example:

- Offer a free sample of your product.
- Offer a free booklet, handbook or eBook.
- Offer a free CD, DVD, digital audio or video.
- Offer a free estimate with valuable recommendations.
- Offer a free ticket to a seminar where you'll be speaking.
- Offer a free newsletter subscription.
- Offer a free initial consultation.
- Offer a free class on how to use the product—on-site or online. Home Depot does this really well on-site.

Cost:
Once again, maybe a free sample or two.

DEVELOP A POWERFUL, BENEFIT-ORIENTED SOUND BITE

Write a two-to-four sentence "commercial" about your company that you can recite at any given moment. You never know when the guy standing next to you in the elevator might ask, "What do you do for a living?" Having a handy sound bite in your pocket allows you to speak intelligently, confidently and send a well-crafted, benefit-oriented message. You never know—the recipient of your message might just need what you have to offer. And you've landed a new customer without having to "sell."

Cost: Maybe two or three brain cells.

Some examples: "I help people add value to their homes. I hunt down the best quality plants and sell them at the corner of Fourth and Main, and I consult on garden plans." (*plant store owner*)

"My name is _____. I'm a Certified Public Accountant and I save businesses a lot of money." (*CPA*)

My sound bite for my speaking business is, "I'm America's Shoestring Budget Coach and my books and seminars teach entrepreneurs, small business owners, non-profit organizations, performers and self-employed independent contractors how to save a ton of money on marketing and advertising."

DEVISE CREATIVE CONTESTS AND SWEEPSTAKES

Contests and sweepstakes are a great way to appeal to a large audience. And if the prize is grand—or even just unique—your contest may attract media interest. The key is to always give away something that will be perceived as valuable. Giving away something that you manufacture or produce has the added bonus of letting people test your product. And don't forget to distribute a press release announcing your contest or sweepstakes.

Cost: The cost of a prize—but with the right connections in your town, you can probably get a prize for free.

CHAPTER 6
GET
INVOLVED

NETWORKING

Business is personal. The easiest—and quickest—way to promote your business is to forge strong personal relationships with people in your business community.

- Local Chamber of Commerce events
- Local business associations
- Local and national charities
- Networking groups
- Trade shows specific to your business

To understand how to network effectively you must first understand that networking is not just handing your business card out to everyone in the room. It's not a hit-and-run, quick-sell scheme. In fact, it's not *selling* at all.

Always collect more cards than you hand out. Ask open-ended questions and listen more than you speak. Perfect your short "what you do" sound bite.

Get involved in everything you can. Get appointed to special committees. Earn a seat on an organization's Board of Directors or at least their Board of Advisors. Attend the meetings and contribute. And keep coming back. Once you've made a good contact keep the connection alive. Offer a hot lead. Recommend a favorite vendor. Send an article that you believe your contact will benefit from reading. Or better yet, send them a story where they are featured in a magazine or newspaper and sign it offering congratulations.

But offer these favors without expecting a return. Think of networking as planting a seed. You won't see results overnight but the long-term benefits are well worth the wait.

At my graphic design firm, Green Room Design & Advertising, I forged relationships with business owners in my local Chamber of Commerce, which ultimately led to invitations to host two Installation dinners. Each of these dinners had an audience of around 500 business owners, which translated to more than 1,000 potential clients. At the dinner I was introduced as the owner of Green Room Design & Advertising—a free plug. Then to top it off, I won the "Small Business of the Year Award." Guess what? Within a few short days I had acquired about a dozen new clients.

Cost:
Your time.

PARTICIPATE IN COMMUNITY SERVICE EVENTS

There's no better way to get noticed in your community than to participate in a non-profit organization's annual charity event—whether as the chairperson or a volunteer. You'll be giving back to the community and you'll be viewed as a community leader. You and your company will earn instant respect and admiration. People do business with people they respect and admire.

Cost: You're a volunteer. Please don't pay anything to be a volunteer.

JOIN THE ASSOCIATIONS OF YOUR CUSTOMERS AND COMPETITORS

By joining business associations you'll enhance your visibility, expand your business contacts and have opportunities to impact the industry or profession that's important to you. Seek out associations that are relevant to your peers, customers, and yes—your competitors.

You can turn your competitors into business allies at least some of the time. When you can't convince your customer that your Brand X is what he wants, send him to the best Brand Y dealer in town. You'll gain credibility, and most often, the Brand Y dealer will return the favor. You'll also get to know how your competitors do business.

Cost:
Most associations have a nominal registration fee.

CHAPTER 7
BECOME AN EXPERT

PICK A NICHE AND GROW RICH

Find a need and fill it. Remember both halves of the saying "Jack of all trades—and master of none." You and your business cannot be all things to all people. Focus on your special niche and stay with it. Continue to expand your knowledge of your own field of expertise.

Here is a perfect example of picking a niche: If you want to get into the fishing industry, don't target "Fishing"—it is way too general. Focus instead on "Fishing Lures." By narrowing down the size of the market you immediately gain a huge advantage over the larger companies. It will be easier for you to build close relationships with your customers and you will become an instant expert in your field.

Cost:
To pick a niche costs zilch.

TEACH A CLASS

Colleges are always on the lookout for professionals or "experts" for guest lectures and special speaking events. Being associated with colleges and universities gives you instant credibility, and it's a great way to attract local media attention. Once again, free exposure.

Community colleges offer short evening courses. You might offer a course in "Record Keeping for Tax Purposes" or "Planning Your Landscape" or whatever touches your area of expertise. Don't neglect high schools. Those kids will be your customers in a few years.

Offer one-evening courses at your place of business. Surprisingly, more people will be eager to attend if you charge a small fee ($10 - $25) than if you offer it for nothing.

Promote yourself as an expert source and let local media know you're available for interviews. Listen to radio talk shows and call in to offer your opinion when the topic is within your realm of expertise.

Cost: Again, just your time.

SPEAK AT SEMINARS, MEETINGS & WORKSHOPS

Volunteer to speak at seminars, workshops and meetings—offer to be a keynote speaker, panel member or seminar host. Local business associations such as your Chamber of Commerce usually offer plenty of opportunities.

Since you are keeping up in your area of expertise you won't have much trouble finding a topic that will be of general interest. Write your speech in advance and practice it often. Include humor and anecdotes to keep your audience listening.

If you are worried about your speaking skills join Toastmasters International. Their tried-and-true program will have you speaking like a pro in a few months.

Cost: They should be paying you, but if you volunteer you look like the hero, and inevitably that will turn into more clients and more money in your pocket.

WRITE A BOOK

There is no quicker way to become an expert in your field than to write a book. But most people think that writing a book is one of the most difficult things in the world to do.

It is not!

You don't have to write the Great American Novel, or a 300-pound comprehensive treatment. Do what I did—trim the fat and the fluff and write a smaller book. Pick a topic that has something to do with your small business—remember, you're marketing as well. Aim for an 80- to 96-page book. If you write about four or five pages a day you'll be finished in a few weeks.

And don't worry about being perfect or you'll never finish it. Just write the book and get it printed. If after it's printed you realize you forgot to put something very important in your book, just write Part 2.

To start writing a book, imagine you are talking to a friend. What would you need to say about the topic? Jot down all your ideas. Now organize them into a working outline. Expand on the ideas one by one. If you find you need more information do some research on the Internet—but do not plagiarize.

Be sure to include an author's biography with career information about you that is relevant to the topic. Include your business and contact information.

Before you take your book to the printer have someone else read it. Ask them to mark passages they don't understand. Then you can rewrite to make everything clear. Read the book aloud; you'll notice the kind of mistakes a spell-checker doesn't find.

Cost: Writing is just your time. You can get a book like mine printed for less than a dollar each if you print enough copies. If you have no budget, make it an eBook where the printing cost is ZERO. You can even offer your eBook on sites like Lulu.com and Amazon.com.

CHAPTER 8
CORRESPONDENCE

GO ABOVE AND BEYOND

Seems obvious, doesn't it? But you'd be surprised at how many businesses don't realize the value of going above and beyond. Sometimes going above and beyond can be a differentiating attribute in itself and a compelling competitive advantage.

Here are some ideas for going above and beyond:

- Send a thank-you note immediately after any purchase.
- Send a free newsletter—monthly, bi-monthly, or quarterly.
- Offer an item related to their purchase within a few weeks after the purchase.
- Conduct a customer-only contest. Guarantee that the prize will be awarded to an existing customer only. Make sure the contest form has a questionnaire and an area where you can get all their contact information, including their birthday.
- Send a birthday card.
- Make a time-limited offer to your customers first and inform them that the offer will not be available to the general public until a week later.

Cost:
A postage
stamp or two.

SEND HANDWRITTEN THANK YOU NOTES

As touched on earlier in going above and beyond, the thank you note is becoming rarer and rarer—handwritten thank you notes are practically extinct. It's a great opportunity to tell your customers how much you appreciate their business or a referral. Your customer will remember that you took the time to send a handwritten note. You've just made a lasting impression.

When a supplier or sales rep goes out of their way to help you, send a thank you note to the person who helped you, and to their boss.

Cost: The price of a piece of paper, an envelope and a stamp.

ALWAYS FOCUS ON GETTING TESTIMONIALS

For some strange reason most small business don't focus on getting testimonials. It's one of the easiest things to do and it's free.

Always ask for a testimonial from a satisfied customer. Include the testimonial on your website, in your flyers, ads, direct mail campaigns, sales letters, and even on the back of your business cards.

If you can, try to make sure the testimonial is results-based. For example: "After using your new marketing system I applied what I learned and immediately made an extra $10,000 this month."

TURN YOUR VOICE MAIL MESSAGE INTO A FREE ADVERTISING TOOL

Instead of just recording your hours of operation, why not turn your outgoing message into a mini commercial? Include your sound bite. Consistently reinforce your company's key message and benefits in *all* your printed and electronic materials. At my professional theatre, we announced our upcoming shows on our outgoing phone message—free promotion.

Cost: If this costs you anything, close your business today.

WHO'S ANSWERING YOUR PHONE?

It matters. Your employee's phone-answering skills can make or break your business. I cannot overemphasize the importance of this one little thing. The person answering your phone is the voice of your company, and in some cases, will be a prospect's first impression of your company.

Make phone etiquette a part of your training program. It's a subject not taught in schools so don't expect even employees with experience to know what to do. Your phone should never ring more than three times before someone answers it. Your employees should have a cheerful attitude over the phone, even when someone is complaining. Yes, you will have to tell them that the customer is always right.

Cost: You're already paying their salary, so this is also free.

LOVE YOUR TELEPHONE

If you're stressed, before you answer the phone, take a couple of deep breaths to clear your mind. (And also to make sure you don't sound breathless.) Then you can give all your attention to the call.

Be sure you have a notepad and pencil near every phone so you can write down orders, take a message, or jot down the solution to a problem.

Smile while talking on the telephone. People will "hear" you smiling! Remember: People do business with people they like.

Cost:
Absolutely free.

CHAPTER 9
MEDIA

USE PRINT MEDIA TO PROMOTE YOUR BUSINESS

No, having your ad in the Yellow Pages is not enough. Not even close. With a little creativity you can expand your print advertising without greatly expanding your budget. Research the costs of advertising in regional editions of national magazines. Look into buying remnant magazine space; you may be astonished how inexpensively you can advertise in high-prestige magazines. Advertise in inexpensive one-page newsletters that have high circulation numbers.

Local newspaper advertising is obviously much less expensive than national magazines and can be very useful if you have a local target market. Niche magazines, on everything from log homes to collecting baseball cards, have directories of businesses for each state. You can be listed for a small fee. You will be amazed at how much response such a listing can bring you.

Write good articles or a weekly column about topics in your realm of expertise and submit them to local publications. You can achieve "expert" status within your community in a few short weeks. When you gain confidence you might submit an article to a trade or professional magazine.

Cost: Prices vary from free to relatively expensive for a local publication. And if you have the budget for a national magazine look into remnant magazine space.

SHOW OFF YOUR PRESS CLIPPINGS

Press clippings are gold. Yesterday's newspaper may be dead and gone but good publicity can live forever. And the best part is clips are free and far more powerful than any ad you'll ever buy.

Distribute your clip reprints in mailings. Include them in your press kit, brochure package, and sales rep kits. Reproduce them on your website. Frame them and display them in your lobby.

If your local paper features you or your business in a staff-written piece consider enlarging it a bit, the way restaurants blow up favorable reviews.

Cost: Pretty much free—just the cost of copies and frames.

SEND PRESS RELEASES FOR JUST ABOUT EVERYTHING

Press releases are a good way to launch a relationship with newspapers and Internet news hubs. Journalists have a certain number of column inches to fill every day and you never know when they might just consider you newsworthy.

Use press releases to distribute important announcements to mass media. Examples include:

- Opening your business
- New product or service
- Giveaways, contests or sweepstakes
- New employees

Be sure to fax press releases in enough time to meet newspaper deadlines. Always include your name, phone number and e-mail address as a "contact." Put who,

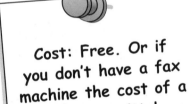

Cost: Free. Or if you don't have a fax machine the cost of a fax transmittal.

what, when, where in the first sentence or two. Then explain more fully. Write about the most important thing first and the less important details later in the piece.

I asked Academy Award nominee Debra Winger to come to my theatre and perform a book reading. I'll bet you can imagine how much free press I generated from those appearances!

CHAPTER 10
PARTNERSHIPS

FORM STRATEGIC ALLIANCES WITH COMPANIES WHO SHARE YOUR TARGET MARKET

Partners come in all shapes and sizes. Joining forces with suppliers—even customers—can be a powerful marketing tactic. Piggyback on another company's mailing. Insert your flyer in your partner's mailing to its association members. Write an article for your partner's newsletter. In addition to gaining new prospects you'll save the postage and production costs. Scout partners at trade shows. Share leads. Form strategic alliances.

My theatre partnered with our local garbage collection company—now that's thinking outside the box. Included in the monthly trash bill was a small insert promoting the shows in my upcoming season. All I had to do in exchange was give them two comp seats to every show that season and a sponsorship ad in our program. My insert landed in the hands of more than 60,000 people. And I didn't pay a dime for postage.

Cost: I got the insert included in a gang run, so the cost of printing 60,000 inserts was less than $200. And here's the best part—a corporate sponsor picked up the cost of the printing because I built that cost into their sponsorship fee.

SCOUT SPONSORSHIP OPPORTUNITIES

Generate free publicity by sponsoring a local community-service event. Evaluate sponsorship opportunities the same way you evaluate all marketing opportunities: Look for direct tie-ins to your products and target market. Bear in mind, the "currency" for sponsorships doesn't necessarily have to be dollars and cents. You can donate products or services.

Sponsoring a large event as a Title Sponsor can be very costly, but you can also sponsor a portion of an event for a lot less. For example, if you wanted to be the Title Sponsor for a local charity golf tournament it might cost you about $25,000. But if you just sponsor one of the holes it may only run you about $250. Yes you get less exposure, but you do get exposure.

Cost: Could be a little, could be a lot. You choose.

LOOK FOR TIE-IN MARKETING OPPORTUNITIES

Tie-in marketing—creating an association between the products or services of your company to another company—can be incredibly powerful. Tie-ins can create instant brand awareness and differentiation, generate media buzz and build powerful, mutually beneficial long-term marketing relationships. A clever tie-in lets your company join the dialogue your prospects were already having. In fact, tie-ins that revolve around the topics that are currently hot in the collective consciousness can be particularly effective.

Forging alliances with major national corporations that have logical tie-ins to your product or services can be incredibly profitable. But don't limit your alliances to household names. Look for opportunities among:

- Suppliers and service providers; for example, beverage vendors, cable providers, Internet service providers
- Businesses that sell different products, but target the same customer base you do. This tactic can be particularly effective when your products are complimentary.
- Geographically related businesses. Businesses on your street, in your city or state.
- Businesses you patronize frequently: Banks, stores, etc.

- Private investors and venture capitalists
- Local celebrities
- Local sporting events, concerts, and other entertainment venues

At my theatre, I was jokingly referred to as the barter king. I learned that I could barter just about anything simply because people wanted to be part of the theatre experience. I often gave away free show tickets in exchange for products or services the theatre needed.

Cost: Again nothing—except samples of your product or services.

GET A COACH

I'm sure you've made lots of resolutions to do this or that as you continue to read this book. You've probably jotted down some notes or even taken time to make an action list. But life happens. Every day you have customers, suppliers and personnel to deal with. It's so easy to say, "I'll get to it when I'm less busy."

You will never, ever be "less busy." Bottom line—if you want to be successful you need someone to hold you accountable. Someone to make sure you actually write your marketing plan, get active in that civic organization, buy stationery for thank you notes.

A business coach not only helps you develop your plans and figure out how to make them reality, he or she checks to make sure you act on them.

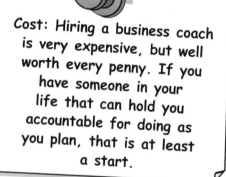

Cost: Hiring a business coach is very expensive, but well worth every penny. If you have someone in your life that can hold you accountable for doing as you plan, that is at least a start.

CHAPTER 11

MAKE MONEY WHILE YOU SLEEP

ENLIST AN ARMY OF AFFILIATES TO SELL YOUR PRODUCT

Offering an affiliate program is a cost-effective way to recruit an army of free sales reps who will generate leads or sales for you in exchange for a commission. There are scads of affiliate marketers out there scouring the Internet every day for new products and services to promote on their websites. You can run your own affiliate tracking program, outsource it to an affiliate tracking service, or establish an account through affiliate brokers such as Commission Junction (www.cj.com), LinkShare (www.linkshare.com), or ShareASale (www.shareasale.com).

Cost:
You should only
make money
doing this.

TURN YOUR CUSTOMERS INTO SALES REPS

In other words—referrals. Once you have rapport with a customer don't be shy about asking them if they know anyone else that could use your product or service. And ask them if they have media contacts that might be interested in covering your company.

The top salespeople at any company are on top because of referrals. When you have a referral to a potential customer you begin from a position of trust because a mutual friend likes your products or services. Sales to referred customers take less time, so the top salesmen have time to prospect for still more sales.

Remember to send a thank you note to the person who gave you the referral.

Cost:
Free, once again.

APPENDIX A

There are so many different ways to write a Business Plan and there are many Internet sites that can help walk you through the process. The U.S. Small Business Association (www.sba.gov) is a great resource for everything you need to know about starting a small business and they have numerous examples of Business Plans. A basic Business Plan should include these key components...

The Executive Summary
The Executive Summary summarizes the key elements of your entire Business Plan. Though this section appears first in the Business Plan, it's actually written last.

Company Description
What business are you in and what will your company do? Include your mission statement, your company's goals and objectives, your business philosophy, and your company's strengths and core competencies.

Products and Services
Describe in depth your products and services. What are the pricing, fee and leasing structures of your products and services?

The Industry
An overview of your company's industry sector. Include industry trends, major players in your industry, and total industry sales projections. This section should also summarize your company's positioning within the industry.

Market Analysis

An examination of the primary target market for your product or service. Includes geographic and demographic analyses, as well as the needs of your target markets and an explanation of how these needs are currently being met.

Competitive Analysis

An investigation of your direct and indirect competitors that includes an assessment of each company's competitive advantage and an analysis of how you will overcome any market entry barriers.

Marketing Plan

A detailed presentation of your sales strategy, pricing strategy, proposed advertising and promotional plan, and your product's or service's benefits, features and differentiating attributes.

Management And Ownership

An outline of your company's tax and legal structure plus the organization of your management team.

Operating Plan

A description of your business' physical location, facilities and equipment, employee qualifications, inventory requirements and suppliers, and any other applicable operating details, such as a description of your manufacturing process.

Financial Plan

A description of your funding requirements, detailed financial statements, and a financial statement analysis.

Appendices And Exhibits

Any additional information that will help establish credibility for your business idea, such as marketing studies, product photographs, and/or contracts or other pertinent legal agreements.

APPENDIX B

There are also many different ways to write a Marketing Plan. Once again, the U.S. Small Business Association (www.sba.gov) is a great resource for Marketing Plans as well. A basic Marketing Plan should include these key components...

Products and Services
A detailed description of your products and services, including special features and benefits.

Demographics
What is your geographic marketing area, local or national?

Competition
Includes who your competition is, how you differ from them, and the level of demand for the product or service.

Pricing Strategy
How much are your products and services?

Promotions
Includes your promotional methods as well as your competitors.

Distribution
How will you get your products and services to your customers?

Customers

Define who your customers are—age, sex, income and neighborhood, what their patterns are, what they value most, and what they value least.

Advertising

How will your customers learn about your products and services?

Marketing

What marketing methods have you used to communicate your message and which of them have been most effective? What methods will you use in the future?

Cost Comparison

Includes cost compared to sales, and cost per customer.

Marketing Budget

How much will you allocate to your entire marketing campaign?

Test Marketing

What methods will you use to test your marketing ideas and to measure the effectiveness of your marketing campaign?

Objectives

What are your overall objectives to communicate your message, create an awareness of your product or service, motivate customers to buy and increase sales, or other specific targets?